Presented to

With love, from

Date

Paste in a photo of you and baby

**Children are a gift from the Lord.**

*—Psalm 127:3*

# There's a Brand-New Baby at Our House and...

I'm the Big Sister!

Written by Susan Russell Ligon

Illustrated by Meghan List & Susan Skinner

Tommy NELSON

A Division of Thomas Nelson Publishers
Since 1798

Mfg. by LEO
Heshan, China
August 2010 / PO# 110405

Published in Nashville, Tennessee, by Tommy Nelson®, a Division of Thomas Nelson, Inc.

Designed by Susan Skinner

ISBN 0-8499-7794-0 (hardcover)
ISBN 10: 1-4003-0966-2 (trade paper)
ISBN 13: 978-1-4003-0966-5 (trade paper)

Printed in China

10 LEO 9 8 7 6 5 4 3

For big brother Daniel and
little brother Andrew.
I love the way you love each other.

— S.R.L.

# I'm the Big Sister!

There's a brand-new baby at our house, and . . . I'm the big sister!

My name is _____.

My birthday is _____, and I am now _____ years old.

I am _____tall, and I weigh _____ pounds.

Big Sister Face                          Baby Face

**I praise you because you made me in an amazing and wonderful way.**

—*Psalm 139:14*

WA WAAA WAAA WAAA! NOW MY BABY NEEDS A NAP.

AHHH GOO BABA.

IT'S BABY'S PLAYTIME!

I'M A GREAT BIG SISTER.

WOW! I'M A LOT BIGGER THAN MY BABY!

BIG GIRL

(Draw a picture or paste in a photo of yourself)

IT'S BABY'S PLAYTIME!

I'M A GREAT BIG SISTER.

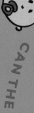

(Draw a picture or paste in a photo of baby.)

**Every perfect gift is from God.**
—James 1:17

# Getting to Know Baby

My baby's name is _____.

My baby was born on _____,

weighs _____,

and is _____ long.

I think my baby looks like _____

_____

_____

_____!

THIS IS A PICTURE OF ME WHEN I WAS A BABY.

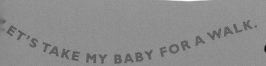

## Getting Ready for Baby

There is a lot to do to get ready for my baby.

I helped Mommy clean up _____,

get out _____,

and buy a new _____.

(Color or paste a piece of your special blankee here.)

WHEN I WAS A BABY,
MY FAVORITE BLANKET
LOOKED LIKE THIS.

Daddy says my baby will need to borrow some of the things that I used when

I was small.  I can't wait to share my _____

and my _____

and my _____.

## Hands and Feet

My baby has tiny hands and feet,

just perfect for playing

"This Little Piggy Went to Market."

Mommy says I used to have tiny

"piggies," too.

*Place baby's handprint here.*

*Place baby's footprint here.*

THIS LITTLE PIGGY CRIED "WEE, WEE, WEE!" ALL THE WAY HOME.

Place your handprint here.

Place your footprint here.

# All About Me

Mommy and Daddy say there is no one else just like me.

My eyes are _____.

My hair is _____.

People say I look like _____.

My baby _____ look like me.
(does/doesn't)

My baby has _____ hair and

_____ eyes.

MY BABY SMILES WHEN I MAKE FUNNY FACES!

(Draw or paste in a picture of yourself.)

I CAN MAKE FUNNY FACES IN THE MIRROR!

BEING THE BIG SISTER IS AWESOME!

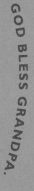

My Baby

Me

Mommy

Daddy

Grandma
(Mommy's Mommy)

Grandpa
(Mommy's Daddy)

Grandma
(Daddy's Mommy)

Grandpa
(Daddy's Daddy)

(Fill in your family tree.)

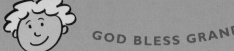 GRANDMA. GOD BLESS GRANDPA.  THANK YOU, GOD

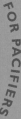 FOR PACIFIERS.

# My Family

My baby and I have a very special family.

I made my family tree with blocks. Other special people in my family are

_____     _____

_____     _____

_____     _____

_____     _____

_____     _____

 GOD BLESS BABY.

 THANK YOU, GOD, FOR APPLE TREES.

> **As for me and my family, we will serve the Lord.**
>
> —*Joshua 24:15*

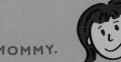 GOD BLESS MOMMY. GOD BLESS DADDY.  I LOVE APPLES.

# A Shower of Gifts

Lots of people brought presents for my baby.

Some people even brought me gifts, too.

It was fun to get

_____ from _____

_____ from _____

_____ from _____

_____
from
_____

_____
from
_____

I GOT A FUN CARD IN THE MAIL TODAY.

MY BABY GOT A LOT OF GREAT PRESENTS, TOO.

_____

from

_____

I LIKE TO HELP MY BABY OPEN PACKAGES!

**A generous person will be blessed.**

—Proverbs 22:9

I LIKE HOLDING MY BABY. A BWOOO DABAAA BWAAAP!

MY BABY THINKS I'M THE BEST BIG SISTER EVER!

A BWOOO DABAAA BWAAAP!

(Draw a picture or paste in a photo of you holding baby.)

 MY BABY SAYS I'M A GREAT HELPER.  GOO BAA WOOOP.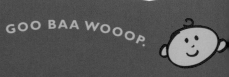

## Holding Baby

The first time Mommy and Daddy let me hold

_____
(baby's name)

was _____

_____

_____

_____

_____.

I LIKED IT WHEN

MY BABY GRABBED
MY FINGER REALLY TIGHT.

My baby felt very _____

and smelled like _____.

# Favorite Things to Do

Some of the special things I like to do are _____

_____

_____

_____

_____

_____

_____

_____

_____.

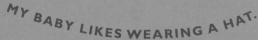
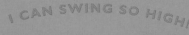

My baby likes to _____

_____

and _____ .

My baby sure sleeps a lot! I'll have to teach _____
(baby's name)

how to _____ and

_____ .

# First Words and Steps

Some of my first words were _____

_____,

and I think my baby's first word will be _____.

Right now my baby is pretty quiet except when _____

_____

_____.

I learned to walk when I was _____ old.

Maybe I can help my baby learn

how to walk! It must get

boring just lying down all of the time.

> We will speak
> the truth with love.
> —*Ephesians 4:15*

# Fun Foods

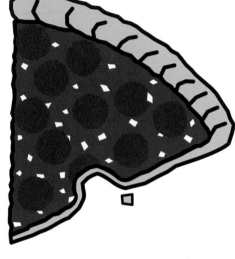

My favorite foods are _____,

_____,

_____,

_____,

_____,

and especially _____!

(baby's name)

likes to eat

_____

_____

_____

_____.

Mommy says my baby is too little to eat what I do!

I can't wait until baby and I can share

_____

_____

_____

_____

_____.

# Bible Stories

The Bible is a very special book that's

filled with stories of people who did

amazing things with God's help.

My favorite Bible story is _____

_____

_____.

**Your word is like a lamp for my feet and a light for my way.**
—Psalm 119:105

A special story in the Bible about a baby is _____

_____

_____

_____.

I'll tell my baby all about it!

GOD TAKES CARE OF LITTLE CHILDREN.

MY BABY CAN MAKE A FUNNY FISH FACE. BOP, BOP, BOP, BOP, BOP.

HERE, KITTY, KITTY, KITTY!

MY BABY CAN MAKE A FUNNY FISH FACE.

BOP BOP

# My Pets

I love animals.  Some of my favorite animal friends are _____

and _____

and _____ .

Right now, my baby's pets are all stuffed animals.

My favorite stuffed animals are _____

_____

_____

_____ .

MY HAMSTER SMELLS FUNNY.

DOGGIES ARE A KID'S BEST FRIEND.

BOP BOP.

(Paste or draw a picture of an animal friend.)

**A friend loves you all the time.**

—*Proverbs 17:17*

the little star

the little star

## Best-Loved Books

I love stories! Some of my favorite books are _____,

_____, and

_____.

When I was a baby, my favorite books were _____

_____.

Daddy and I like to read _____ to baby.

My baby likes books with _____

_____

and _____

_____.

READING MAKES ME SMART!

# Growing Up

I am getting bigger every day.

When I grow up, I want to be a

_____

or a _____

_____

or maybe  a _____

_____

_____

_____

_____.

(Draw or paste a picture of what you want to be when you grow up.)

**Before you were born,
I set you apart for a special work.**

—Jeremiah 1:5

MY BABY IS GOING TO BE A REALLY LOUD SINGER. YEA YEAA YEA!

MY BABY MIGHT DRIVE A FIRE TRUCK.

I'LL BE THE BEST BIG SISTER WHEN I GROW UP.

(Draw or paste a picture of what you think baby might grow up to be.)

My baby is really good at

_____.

I think _____ might grow up to be a _____.
(baby's name)

CAN I BE A TEACHER WHEN I GET BIG? I LIKE TEACHING MY BABY.

# Favorite Toys and Collections

The toys I love to play with the most are

_____

_____

and _____

_____

_____

_____.

I gave my baby a

_____.

My baby really loves it!

Right now, my baby

seems to be collecting

_____.

_____
(rattles, bottles, pacifiers, diapers)

I like to collect _____

_____

_____

_____.

HOW MANY MORE DAYS UNTIL MY BIRTHDAY?

CAN I STAY UP LATE

I LIKE ALL THE PRETTY CHRISTMAS LIGHTS.

I MADE A VALENTINE FOR MY BABY.

(Paste a card or photo, or draw a picture of your favorite holiday or special day.)

I GOT A COOL CARD IN THE MAIL.

DA DA DA DA DA DA.

I GOT A COOL CARD IN THE MAIL.

# Holidays and Special Days

My favorite holiday is _____.

On this special day, I like to _____ and

_____, and I like to eat

_____.

On my birthday, I like to

_____

_____

_____.

My favorite party was

_____

_____

_____.

I CAN'T WAIT UNTIL MY BABY'S FIRST BIRTHDAY!

I LIKE ALL THE PRETTY CHRISTMAS LIGHTS.

# Bedtime

At bedtime I like to

brush my teeth and

put on my favorite

_____

_____ .

I sleep with my special

_____

_____ .

AND WAKE US WITH THE MORNING LIGHT. AMEN. NIGHT, NIGHT, MOMMY AND DADDY.

When I say my bedtime prayers, I like to pray for

_____

_____

_____

_____

_____

and, of course, _____!
(baby's name)

**Never stop praying.**
—I Thessalonians 5:17

NIGHT, NIGHT, BABY.

I LOVE YOU.

I CAN COUNT TO TWENTY.

I LEARNED HOW TO WINK!

MY BABY IS LEARNING TO STICK OUT HIS TONGUE.

LOOK AT ME ROLLERSKATE.

(Paste a picture of you doing something new.)

IT'S FUN HELPING MY BABY LEARN.

(Paste a picture of baby doing something new.)

I CAN EAT A COOKIE IN ONE BITE!

LOOK, MOM! NO TRAINING WHEELS

# Learning Every Day

I just learned how to _____

and _____

_____.

Daddy says I am really a big girl.

My baby is learning how to

_____

and _____.

I am so proud of

_____!
(baby's name)

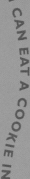

MY BABY SMILES AT ME A LOT. AHH BABA GOODLE DWAP!

MY BABY SMILES AT ME A LOT.  AHH BABA GOODLE DWAP! THAT MEANS —

BEING THE
BIG SISTER IS FUN!

(Draw a picture or paste in a photo of you playing with baby!)

"I WANT TO BE JUST LIKE YOU."  BABA BABA.  MY BABY SAID

# Big Sister and Baby

Mommy and Daddy think I am a great big sister and that

_____ already loves me a lot!
(baby's name)

I can't wait until my baby is older so we can _____,

_____

and _____

_____.

**Love each other.**
—*John 13:34*

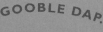

MY BABY SAID, "BIG SISTER!"   GOOBLE DAAAP.   BEING THE BIG SISTER IS FUN!

# Photos and More!

Paste in some of your favorite

photos of you and baby.

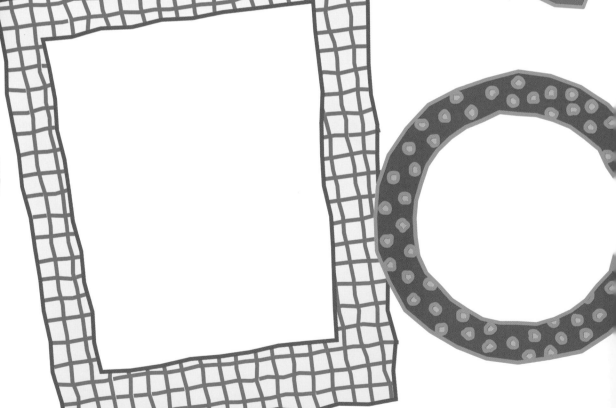

I ALWAYS WANT TO REMEMBER THIS SPECIAL DAY.

LET'S TAKE ANOTHER PICTURE OF ME HOLDING MY BABY.

MAY I TAKE A PICTURE?

MY BABY LOVES ME!

LET'S TAKE ANOTHER PICTURE OF BABY.

I LOVE MY BABY, AND
I LOVE BEING A BIG SISTER!